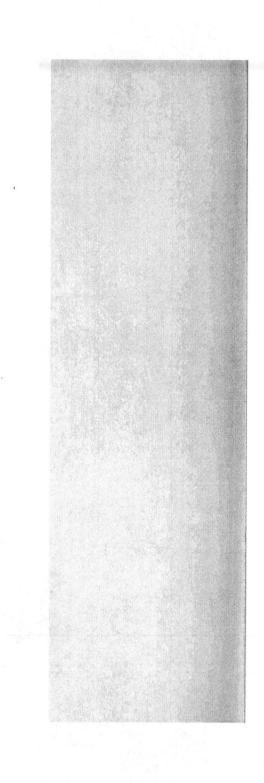

SAINT TARCISIUS

SAINT
TARCISIUS

Written by
MARY R. BERARDI

Illustrated by
G. DE LUCA

ST. PAUL EDITIONS

Long ago, in the year 258 A.D., the mighty Roman Empire was ruled by the Emperor Valerian.

For about five years, the Christians had not been persecuted for their Faith. It seemed a time of peace. But the Prefect Macrian thought!

"Who cares if the common people follow the teachings of that Hebrew, Jesus Christ! It is a religion for poor people. . . . But when the great noblemen and soldiers join it, that is too much!"

Macrian told the Emperor what he had been thinking.

"You are right!" said Valerian. "I must order a persecution of the Christians. It shall begin today! Rome cannot bow to the commandments of the Hebrew, Jesus."

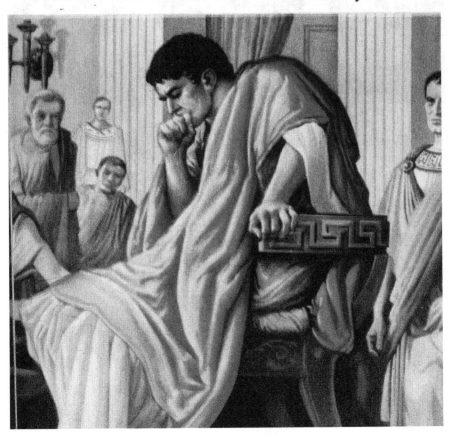

And so Valerian ordered that anyone who declared himself a Christian should be punished with death. The only ones who would be set free would be those who denied Christ and honored the gods of Rome.

That very night, Pope Sixtus II called the Christians together in the catacombs.

"My brothers and sisters and beloved children in our Lord Jesus Christ," he began. "As you already know, the persecution has begun once again! And I want you to know also that some of the faithful have already been taken into the cold, dark prison. Let us pray for them!"

The persecution grew worse every day. The hunt for the Christians grew more and more cruel. Into their homes

8

went the Emperor's soldiers and dragged the Christians away. The prisons were packed. And every evening when the sun was setting, the condemned Christians lifted their voices in hymns to God. The beautiful sound of their singing floated up from the damp, dark underground jails.

One evening a young boy was walking up and down near the horrible prisons. His name was Tarcisius and he was the son of the Senator Tarsente.

With his heart full of pity, Tarcisius was listening to the singing of the condemned Christians. Going up closer, he knelt down by the barred windows, and stayed there, listening. How sorry he felt for the poor prisoners!

Tarcisius returned home late. His governess was waiting for him in the doorway.

"Why so late, Tarcisius? I was worried about you—especially since your father is not at home. He had to go into hiding. They are trying to find him to question him."

"He went into hiding?"

"Yes, Tarcisius, for your sake."

"But, if they find him, he will not deny Christ, will he? He will not betray Him?" the boy asked.

"Oh, no! Now come inside, supper is ready."

It was a sad supper without his father. Tarcisius ate slowly. Suddenly he asked, "I have heard people say that my mother was martyred. Is that right?"

"Yes," replied the governess, "under the Emperor Decian. Your father was going to tell you some day."

"When?"

"When you would be older."

"But I am already old!" said Tacisius. Then he begged, "Please tell me more about my mother."

"Yes, yes, I will, Tarcisius, my boy. Your mother told me that she would be waiting for you in heaven. She loved you very much."

Tarcisius' eyes glowed at the kind old woman's words. "Tell me more," he begged.

"Your mother was young and beautiful, Tarcisius, and although she loved you so much, she was faithful to Christ." The governess went on with her story. Then, later that evening, she and Tarcisius went down into the catacombs.

The Pope was facing them, seated on a great stone chair, the chair of Peter. His face was white and marked by suffering, but his bright eyes shone with piety and tender love.

"Brothers, many of our number will be judged tomorrow," he said. "Their fate is certain—they will all be killed!" Sighs and low moans were heard in the crowd. Quadratus, a tall, strong young man, stepped forward. He was a Roman soldier who had become a follower of Christ. He said, "Holy Father I have seen them! Today I was on guard at the prison. They made me promise to ask you to send them the Bread of Heaven."

"How can we get the Holy Eucharist to them?" sighed Pope Sixtus. "Who will dare to go into the prison? You?"

11

"I cannot," answered Quadratus. "Tomorrow I shall be on guard on the Appian Way."

"Who dares to go on this dangerous mission?" asked the Pope. "Who will take the chance?"

There were shouts of "I!" "I!" "No, I!"

Tarcisius made his way forward through the crowd of people until he was standing before Pope Sixtus.

"Holy Father, send me!" he cried.

"You, Tarcisius—so young?" said Pope Sixtus in surprise. "Why, you are just a boy!"

"Because I am only a boy, no one will pay any attention to me," answered Tarcisius hopefully.

12

Pope Sixtus looked at him carefully for a long moment. In Tarcisius' eyes he saw a strong, ardent desire to carry Jesus to the prisoners.

"All right," he decided. "You shall be the one. I will give the Eucharistic Jesus to you, in this little case."

"I will carry It on my heart," promised Tarcisius joyfully. "I will hold It tight like this! I am ready to die to keep unbelievers from seeing It."

The next day, some schoolmates of Tarcisius were sitting on a pile of stones, on the Appian Way. With them was Fabian, the little friend of Tarcisius.

"Fabian, where is Tarcisius?" asked one of the boys. "How come your protector is not here?"

"Oh, he will come. He always comes to play."

"Yes, and we will have some stone-throwing," said another boy named Mark. "I cannot wait. Here is a nice pile of stones handy for us, too. Somebody will have a hard job piling them up, afterwards!" He laughed.

The other pagan boys laughed loudly with him. They were afraid of the bully Mark and always did what he told them to do.

The minutes slipped by, yet still there was no sign of Tarcisius.

Mark grew impatient. He wanted to begin the game of throwing stones.

"Tarcisius is taking his time to come," said Fabritius.

"He will come and he will win the stone-throwing game, too," cried Fabian. "He is the best player just as he is the best in school."

14

"He was," said Mark. "Lately he is always sleepy. His head rolls from one side to the other . . . like this!" The boys laughed at him.

Fabritius said, "The teacher has begun to notice it, too."

"Maybe Tarcisius does not feel well," Fabian answered to defend his friend. "Anyway, he will beat you just the same. He is a born winner!"

"And what were you born for, to praise him?" asked Mark crossly.

"I like him a lot," replied Fabian. "He treats me like a brother."

He was stopped by Fabritius, who had seen Tarcisius. "Here he comes!"

Tarcisius was coming toward them silently. His arms were pressed firmly to his chest.

"Come to play!" called Mark. The other boys took up the cry: "Come on!"

But Tarcisius answered, "I cannot. I have an errand to do."

"My, how important you think you are!" sneered Mark. "Cut it out! Come on, let's play."

"I cannot really," Tarcisius said firmly. "Let me go. We will play tomorrow."

16

"No," put in Fabritius, "we will play today, right now. Choose your stones."

Again, Tarcisius said, "I cannot, I tell you! I cannot."

"Oh," sighed Mark in disgust, "you are whining like a baby! Come on fellows, form a circle around him. All right now, let us see—why have you got your arms pressed against your chest? What are you hiding?"

"I do not have to tell you," said Tarcisius. "I cannot tell you."

"Smarty!" sneered Fabritius.

Mark kept up his questioning. "Who *are* you going to tell, Tarcisius? The Emperor's eagles, maybe?"

"Maybe."

"Oh, this is too much," snapped Mark. "All right now. . . ."

In his heart, Tarcisius prayed, "Please, Jesus, make my arms as strong as iron! I will press You close to me. I will defend You!"

How the poor boy was suffering! His heart was pounding, and his eyes were nearly blinded with tears. His face was as white as a sheet. The boys crowded around him. The circle grew smaller.

"We have had enough, Tarcisius," warned Mark. "I will give you time to tell us. I will count to three. One. . . ."

Tarcisius prayed silently, "Oh, Lord, Lord, help me!"

"Two!" said Mark.

"Mark, stop it!" cried Tarcisius. "Let me go, Mark. I will give you my bow and arrows, all of them. I will give you anything you want, but please let me continue on my errand!"

"It is no use, Tarcisius!" yelled Mark. "You are hiding something and we are going to find out what it is! I will

17

start counting just once more." Glaring at Tarcisius, he began, "One, two. . . ."

"No!" cried Tarcisius.

"I will repeat it!" Mark's eyes were flashing angrily. "Two. . . .

"Just a second, Mark," said Fabritius. "Fellows, listen to me. I just had an idea."

"I get it!" shouted Mark, in wicked glee. "I had the same idea myself. Tarcisius must be a Christian. And maybe he is carrying around his neck the mysteries!" By that word Mark meant the Holy Eucharist. "Yes, the mysteries! the mysteries!" shouted the other pagan boys.

18

Mark glared at Tarcisius and demanded, "Did you make up your mind, Tarcisius? I said two and—and—"

"I said no, and I meant it!" cried Tarcisius.

"Leave him alone!" pleaded Fabian.

"No, no, Mark, go ahead!" yelled Fabritius.

Tarcisius prayed earnestly, "King of Martyrs, I beg You, don't let me be separated from You. I would rather die!"

"Three!" shouted Mark.

There was a scramble, and several voices shouting, "Give it to him! Give it to Tarcisius! Hit him!"

Tarcisius fell to the ground and like wild beasts, the boys jumped on top of him. Yet his arms stayed crossed over the Mysteries like two iron bands.

With a great effort, he struggled to his feet and was able to run a few steps.

"Grab some stones!" yelled Fabritius. "Give it to him!"

They did just that. One after another, stones struck him from all sides, until there was not a part of his poor body that was not bleeding.

Yet, somehow or other, he was able to stumble on, until one stone struck his forehead. Then Tarcisius fell.

"Tarcisius! Tarcisius!" sobbed Fabian in terror. "Leave him alone, you bullies!"

But Mark urged them on, "Come on, boys, let's get him and see these 'mysteries'."

Just then Fabritius yelled, "Look out! A soldier is coming!"

"He is coming right this way, too," put in another boy. "Let's run!" In an instant, they were gone.

Only Fabian did not run away. He stayed close beside his dear friend, who was suffering terribly.

"Jesus," murmured Tarcisius. "I am dying, but I defended You. Forgive the boys, forgive them!"

Meanwhile, the soldier had come near. It was Quadratus, the Christian. As soon as he caught sight of poor Tarcisius lying on the ground, he exclaimed in horror:

"Poor little fellow! What did they do to you?" Then, seeing Fabian, he asked sharply, "What are you doing here?"

"I am Tarcisius' friend. I love him," wept Fabian, "I did not throw stones at him. Let me stay here, near him."

"Tarcisius, open your arms," Quadratus urged tenderly, bending over the boy.

"No," whispered Tarcisius. "I will not open my arms. Bring me to Pope Sixtus. I will give my treasure—Jesus—only to him."

"Are you suffering much?" asked Quadratus, gently raising Tarcisius' head.

"Yes, very much," Tarcisius gasped, "but that does not matter. Nobody touched Jesus. He is here, right here with

22

me." He was breathing hard, struggling to talk. Suddenly he said, "I already see the Angels. Take me to the Pope!"

"Do not die, Tarcisius! Do not die!" It was Fabian begging tearfully. "You have been like a brother to me."

"I see the Angels," the little martyr repeated. "My Faith is true. And you,"—he gasped for breath—"you, Fabian, do you believe?"

"Yes," declared Fabian, "I believe, Tarcisius. I want to become a Christian, too. Then we can be together again someday."

Quadratus picked up the dying boy in his arms and and carried him to the catacombs.

"Tarcisius," Pope Sixtus whispered gently, after the first shock of seeing the boy in such a pitiful condition. "Tarcisius, Jesus is safe because of your loving sacrifice."

Pressing Jesus in the Eucharist close to his heart, Tarcisius died. Then and only then did his arms fall away from his chest.

This was the beautiful way in which St. Tarcisius, the boy martyr of the Holy Eucharist, died—with his beloved Jesus resting on his heart.

The strong, sweet smell of lilies filled the air at that moment. And Tarcisius' soul—joyful and gay—flew to the throne of God, to the throne of the King Who is waiting for all of us in eternal glory.

Read more about God's Heroes and their exciting, inspiring lives in:

FIFTY-SEVEN

SAINTS

FOR BOYS
AND GIRLS

by the Daughters of St. Paul

Richly Illustrated

Some of the saints in these stories did great things; others did only ordinary things. Yet they all bear a "family resemblance" as Cardinal Cushing calls it—because the likeness of Christ was produced in each one of them. They all spoke with God often in prayer, tried to keep the Ten Commandments perfectly, and were kind and helpful to their fellow men. Every one of us can imitate them in this.

Each of the saints is famous for some particular virtue. Yet, since all of the virtues belong together, growing in one—for instance, charity—helps us to grow in humility and obedience, too. That is why we should try to imitate the virtues of all the saints.

584 pages   Cloth $5.95   Paper $4.95

Order from addresses at the end of this book.

Daughters of St. Paul

IN MASSACHUSETTS
    50 St. Paul's Avenue, Boston, Mass. 02130
    172 Tremont Street, Boston, Mass. 02111
IN NEW YORK
    78 Fort Place, Staten Island, N.Y. 10301
    625 East 187th Street, Bronx, N.Y. 10458
    525 Main Street, Buffalo, N.Y. 14203
IN CONNECTICUT
    202 Fairfield Avenue, Bridgeport, Conn. 06603
IN OHIO
    2105 Ontario St. (at Prospect Ave.), Cleveland, Ohio 44115
    25 E. Eighth Street, Cincinnati, Ohio, 45202
IN PENNSYLVANIA
    1127 South Broad Street, Philadelphia, Pa. 19147
IN FLORIDA
    2700 Biscayne Blvd., Miami, Florida 33137
IN LOUISIANA
    4403 Veterans Memorial Blvd.,
      Metairie, La. 70002
    86 Bolton Avenue, Alexandria, La. 71301
IN MISSOURI
    1001 Pine St. (at North 10th), St. Louis, Mo. 63101
IN TEXAS
    114 East Main Plaza, San Antonio, Texas 78205
IN CALIFORNIA
    1570 Fifth Avenue, San Diego, Calif. 92101
    278 17th Street, Oakland, Calif. 94612
    46 Geary Street, San Francisco, Calif. 94108
IN HAWAII
    1184 Bishop St., Honolulu, Hi. 96813
IN CANADA
    3022 Dufferin Street, Toronto 395, Ontario, Canada
IN ENGLAND
    57, Kensington Church Street, London W. 8, England
IN AUSTRALIA
    58, Abbotsford Rd., Homebush, N.S.W., Sydney 2140,
      Australia